SCL

EARTH

Jaakko Pallasvuo

AM

Arcadia Missa Publications

Unit 6 Bellenden Business Centre
Bellenden Road
Peckham
London SE15 4RF

www.arcadiamissa.com
@ArcadiaMissa
info@arcadiamissa.com

SCORCHED EARTH, 2016

Second Edition, 2016

Design by Zhoe Granger
Illustration by Jaakko Pallasvuo

ISBN: 978-0-9926747-6-2

With additional editing by Arcadia Missa.

Arcadia Missa Publications are available from the gallery, our website and selected stockists.

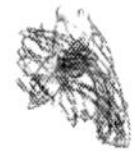

i just wanna communicate clearly again
i think that's why i've been kinda unmotivate
d
becuz i don't feel like i'm reaching ppl
but if i do things in a more blunt artless way it'll work like the how to videos worked
the first lecture is about how i want this guy to play dog in my video
but i'm scared to ask him
and it will be about my problems with the left
and then the second one will be about like
10 reasons to stop playing the art game

He has a handlebar moustache and a wry smile and short beard stubble. A formerly plump body approaching lean. He still looks young. He'll look young for another three years. He will begin to look middle aged.

He has beatroot on his hands. He is smoking a roll-up cigarette. It looks like a joint.

There's a disproportionate amount of scum in the audience. Former art students graduated into alcoholics. Some furious, most already defeated.

They're making vegetarian food with shortcuts, serving it in this artspace, referencing 'relational aesthetics' like it ain't no thing. Like it ain't LOL and a fucking failure. It's like trying to be Christ without performing any actual miracles.

People holding Canon DSLRs. Well-documented feeble gestures. Yves Klein body shapes smushed onto the walls. Art Therapy. 2001-esque anti- globalization rants on tape. Mushroom soup. Oft-repeated thoughts: half embarrassing, half enticing.

One of the drunk audience members is farting into his friend's face . He has pulled down his shorts and exposed his rear. He places his ass closer to his frie nd. The friend is sitting on the asphalt in front of the gallery. Everything happens so fast. This is the second most poetic image of the evening.

The most poetic image is of the first guy's beetroot chunk stained hands holding a hand-rolled cigarette. It's an image in the world, something that vibrates two-dimensionality and is iconic. I try to take a picture of the image but I fail because I don't know how to use this camera. Karl records video and I ask him to send me the video. It must suffice.

I'm so impressed by this unauthored image, this accidental image that justifies all the boring shit and the sense of embarrassment I feel in participating in art activities and the embarrassment I feel just walking down the street or reading a book in a stupid pose or sunbathing when I don't look like the kind of person who should be doing that.

I keep thinking about this work where he would be a dog. Put his improv skills to use. His slight humiliation would be the polar opposite to community building. It's what my mind needs to inhabit these relational relations. Theater is an abuse of power.

Act like a dog, I tell him. I'm not on camera. My voice is slightly distorted. He gets on his knees. What kind of dog are you? I ask him.

He is being filmed in a white space that seems to go on forever. Like the download program in The Matrix. He is on his knees. He is barking. His tongue is out.

His hands are dark purple from intense beetroot-handling. He is smoking a cigarette with those hands. Do you think of people as material? I ask him. What a complex material they are.

In this anxious scenario I don't stop comparing. There's another set of people somewhere. In a big city on another continent. Their degrees are from Ivy League universities or selective liberal arts colleges. They wear Hood By Air and Eckhaus Latta but not to compensate for anything. They just found that stuff on the street or were gifted swag by their stylist BFFs.

There are no contradictions. They are underweight but in shape. They've read everything but have remained young. They party every weekend, live- life-to-the-fullest, but are on track with their meaningful careers come Monday.

They don't get sick.
If they do get sick their friends bring them chicken soup and Gilmore Girls .mp4s, Season 2 for a fit of coughs.

They are marble and vapour. Perfect soul, perfect selfie.

In this anxious scenario I'm on the other side of the Atlantic and am somehow disabled. The nature of this disability keeps changing. In any case it means that I'm stuck. Some deep flaw is holding me back.

My aging parents are tired of taking care of me but have no choice. Otherwise I am alone. I dream of living an independent life, of having an apartment. In this anxious scenario I can't dream bigger than that. Everything is illness and death. Whipped cream mixed with black food coloring.

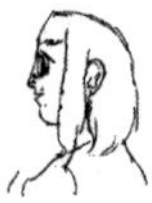

"The most merciful thing in the world, I think, is the inability of the human mind to correlate all its contents. We live on a placid island of ignorance in the midst of black seas of infinity, and it was not meant that we should voyage far. The sciences, each straining in its own direction, have hitherto harmed us little; but some day the piecing
together of dissociated knowledge will open up such terrifying vistas of reality, and of our frightful position therein, that we shall either go mad from the revelation or flee from the light into the peace and safety of a new dark age."
-H.P.Lovecraft

400 years later it would be clear. The fall of the European Union as distant as, and less remarkable than, the fall of the Roman Empire.

Too much lead in the pipes.

Barbarians camped outside the city gates.

#NoNewIdeas

A fine arts degree granted you entry into a growing new social class. The young, urban, educated poor. You had been duped.

Student debt meant a soft slavery. There were faster and slower ways out of debt. The fastest way was to do what was asked of you. They wanted you to lie on your back and let a blob of ice cream melt onto you. They toyed with you in a disinterested way. It wasn't like they had desires you could turn against them. They were on a safari. You were a black panther or some other soon to be obsolete curiosity. There were more of your kind than theirs, but you never formed an alliance. You were a lonely vanilla mess.

"I hope that my success never alters our relationship"

Crumbling infrastructure: riots, murder. We were waiting for the scanners to solve our problems. There were nanobots in our bloodstream. The mutations had already begun. We were glad to be slightly less human.

They were boastful, triumphant; it seemed to both that they had read every book in the world; known every sin, passion, and joy. Civilisations stood round them like flowers ready for picking. Ages lapped at their feet like waves fit for sailing.

- Virginia Woolf, Jacob's Room, published 1922 Reblogged June 4, 2076

Like all smart young people you think you're a fraud and dumb inside.

Everything organised and neat, structure that doesn't trust itself. Obsessive compulsion, getting the details right. Sisyphos painting the exhibition space

white everyday but it's never even and never white enough. Every utopia is a dystopia, she says.

You're a willing fool. You think you're going to win, then you're exhausted by the thought. You're on a double decker bus, it's raining, you haven't eaten properly and have a headache. You think of his beard stubble and what scars he might have. You're without properties.

detailed numbers: debt, amount of rent, unpaid internship, money from parents, real job, prostitution money (or not money; dinners, trips, rent)

He told me he had dreamt about me. In his dream I was trying to cut his artery with a knife. Was it his wrist or his throat that I was aiming for? He didn't say. I felt like I should apologize for all the horrible things I did to him in his dreams.

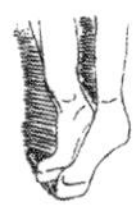

Reality has been augmented. Pure information hovers over us, touches us. I'm more a constellation of data than a being.

Tonight I'm a 35-year old white male. Hairy and overweight but firm. My roundness holds onto traces of past marathons and wrestling matches. I'm pale blonde. I'm so white I'm almost glowing.

Many entities have chosen similar bodies. Eye color and skin tone vary. Fashion choices are identical. This season we dress up as English skinheads. Underneath we are fragile.

He is there. His features are Neanderthal-like. That's the highest compliment I could pay him. I look at him and I'm looking into ancient times. Trees falling onto each other. Pillars and swords and stuff.

I think I might want him so I touch him. It's easy. His skin radiates warmth. Blood surges. Calculations are made. I kiss his ear.

He responds. He slides his hand onto my thigh. His hand moves around. I'm not there anymore. I listen to his sighs while I run image searches. He sees that my eyes have become hooded. When he touches me he is touching a vessel that might hold nothing.

This has begun to happen. I search for a connection that I keep missing. It's biological and authentic. It doesn't work. His body parts only hint at a purpose. I want to go deeper, like, into a soul. Failing that, I prefer images or imagined encounters.

His body, overripe, sweaty, has cooled. He holds his arms to his sides. It's like hugging furniture. It's easier to relate to him now: his absence, his disappointment. I stand on the corner outside of the club and let the wind blow straight through me.

Maybe one can forgive oneself and stop feeling pointless guilt. I carry the weight of a mass of small troubles. The dog is more free than we are. The dog doesn't feel guilt. The dog taking care of the baby.

In the afternoon the rehearsals move to an area with green sofas. We drink coffee and look outside. One of the dancers calls me a parasite, first behind my back and now to my face. It's presented as a joke but holds the sharp edge of truth. I smile and say yes.

There is a need to go outside. It happens easily in this kind of process with no clear aim, I begin to wonder: is there something better I could be doing, like being outside.
The pressure to go outside before the light runs out.

Looking outside at the blue and then there's the green couch.

These super realistic feelings, like in painting, can't give an example. But that the world is clearly defined, has clear lines, is brighter than it is, more clarity in the shapes. Some certain light. I want to see the world for what it is.

The three sisters, isn't their basic problem that they need to be somewhere else? They want to be in the past of somewhere. They want to go to Moscow. This is not an in-depth analysis.

This kind of situation rarely occurs. That one would just talk and everyone listens. It's difficult to stay calm. There is the urge to produce more speech.

I wonder why calm is privileged. Why is it so important to be at ease all the time?

I feel like I should be typing even when they don't talk so it wouldn't be so transparent that I'm writing down what they say. I try to make my expression indifferent and keep my focus on the screen.

After practice yesterday I went to the studio to sing. I have a flu so my voice
sounded weak. It was hard to tolerate. I'm strict towards my voice. It has become this important part of my being, thought and expression. There's such a spectrum of possibilities. I can hear more and more all the time. The voice is becoming a tool.

I have always been ashamed of my soft feminine speaking voice. It's so revealing. When I try to appear more self-assured I begin to speak at a lower range. A basic trick.

The other members of the group have their eyes closed. They are leaning back on the green couches and look like they're asleep. They are in sensitive, receptive states.

There are two segments to the room. An office like area, a kind of boardroom. There is also a black stage like area with mattresses and pillows.

I tell them that yesterday was really useful and interesting. They need to be assured: I'm not judging them.

They are lying on the floor on mattresses, give yourself permission to relax the tape says, repeat to yourself three times: I relax.

They are lying down in the youth area on colorful soft materials. I'm sitting on the conference room side. I feel like a tired adult. I wonder.

Listen to the impulses of the hand, the impulses of the hands to move, follow the impulses if there are any.

Let your hands move slowly, rise or ascend.
Soon open your eyes for a moment and close them again. Continue to move your hands.

Close your eyes again.
Let your hands find their way as far as possible from your heart.
Let your hands rest.

I was looking at him when we were eating. How people are very serious when they focus. I felt old, looking at a young person, looking at someone who is so focused, having the chance to observe another adult, without them being aware of it.

I'm yawning a lot and falling asleep.

The freedom of the person is fundamentally limiting the freedom of the animal.

Alvar Aalto's house. Riihitie, Munkkiniemi. Built in 1936.

2022:

Sunlight through large windows. Houseplants in wooden troughs.

Jaakko Pallasvuo slouching on an uncomfortable black leather sofa. The sofa is nice.

Jaakko Pallasvuo is an odd looking middle-aged person. Either a man or a woman or then not.

Pallasvuo glances at camera.

A documentary is being filmed. Camera explores details of Aalto's house.

Close-up of Pallasvuo's shiny, glittery nails.

Interview

Pallasvuo: I bought this house when I decided to move back from LA. I've always hated modernism but lately it has begun to feel comforting. Like a childhood, not mine though. And this stuff is kinda beautiful.

[image]

Pallasvuo: I always felt misunderstood here, but I'm fine with it. At least right now. I feel like people hate me. But someone has to be that guy. That yuppie art ho.

JAAKKO – a 30 year old blonde woman

MUTE SERVANT - ageless stern-faced androgyne DOG - shiba inu

JAAKKO is sitting on a black leather sofa at Alvar Aalto's house. The house is JAAKKO's new home.

JAAKKO looks on w/ tired expression. JAAKKO smokes an e-cigarette. MUTE SERVANT brings her a glass of water.

JAAKKO is talking to someone sitting behind the camera. JAAKKO in half profile, smiling. A pose familiar from countless TV interviews.

JAAKKO: I've been walking out there in the mist and I've been thinking heavy thoughts. What am I supposed to do in the world? Can I love anyone?

What to do with the knowledge that western culture is a sinking ship? I'm a rat with my money. Living in this mansion. Taking a step back, up north, away from climate change, away from conflict. If Russia attacks from the east I know I won't be able to resist it.. I'll take these paintings and my money and ship them to Switzerland, where the rest of the wealth is. Never a war there. The air is mountain fresh. Bomb shelters to shelter the entire population. Feeling melancholic beauty. Moving my cursor around my desktop. I haven't lived in Finland for a while. Afraid of the distance. Afraid of silence and loneliness and that I'll have to listen to myself and do sports and eat well, that I'll have to take care of myself, and of you. What was I afraid of again?

DOG enters and begs for affection. JAAKKO pats DOG on head, absent- mindedly.

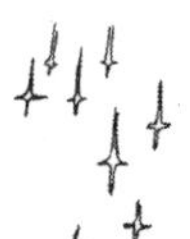

Presenting vigorous critique is a double-edged sword. On one hand: polemic content generates hits. On the other: attacking your peers might cost you their support.

How to appear antagonistic enough to be credible while protecting fragile social relations?

One option is to only commit to vague, general judgements. Don't name names. Maybe your friends will assume that you're talking about everyone except them. The risk is that inexact observations might prove a bore.

Another option is to embrace an aggressive social role: be that guy one loves
to hate. Only go for this strategy if you are a biological male able to project convincing, firm masculinity. This will increase your chances of being understood as an alpha contender. You

don't want to be mistaken for a loudmouth bitch or a bitter faggot.

Critique what you know. Play to an older generation's idea of "youth today". Throw your peers under the bus for being uncritical, listless and cynical. Represent yourself as an untarnished throwback idealist. Maybe Boris Groys will accept your friend request.

Critiquing art institutions demonstrates that you can "think for yourself". You are able to prove the depth of your involvement in their trivial histories. You are clever. You are employable.

Serious criticism mimics academic writing. You don't need scientific methods. Appropriating the terms and aesthetics of research is enough. The purpose is to create an appearance of objectivity and professionalism.

Any reaction is a triumph. Only silence equals death.

"To love without criticism is to be betrayed."
– Djuna Barnes

"Criticism is something we can avoid easily by saying nothing, doing nothing, and being nothing."
- Aristotle 384 B.C.-322 B.C.

The apartment was small. They moved in close proximity to each other.
She was in his line of sight. It was his apartment, one of several. They talked about her getting a place. When they talked about it their body language undermined what they were saying.

At parties he introduced her as his assistant. They weren't fucking yet, but had taken to sleeping in the same bed. She slept facing the radiator and the window above it. He faced the door, the bookcase.

He grabbed her by the waist. It was a possessive move. It played to how people saw them.

The paintings were not a collaboration. Wouldn't it be funny if you.., she began. She pointed at layers, sections, dividers. He would listen and change things. She thought of herself as his editor. What did he think of her?

She felt undervalued. She thought of leaving. She thought of how it would lessen his work and him with it. Then she remembered what it had been like to be unremarkable and alone. Her practice: blank canvases and .psd files that refused her attempts at order, at making sense.

Her intelligence was critical and originated nothing. He produced flaws she could point to. Her own failures were harder to tell apart from triumphs.

The universe makes more sense backwards. Animals retreat into the sea and become single cell organisms. The big bang not as an explosion but a quick compression and ultimate organization of scattered fragments. iPhones turn into dumber cell phones turn into house phones turn into no phones at all. Overpopulation is solved. There's energy again. What would a reverse architecture be? Take something very exact and make it less and less so until it becomes a building.

You move back in with your parents after a couple of short chaotic years abroad. You think it's temporary but then you get sick and your exit strategy fails. You're worried about your health. You don't have money and you feel like a slacker, Generation X. Except those people had Kurt Cobain and each other. They had sweaty nights on cold beaches, busted acoustic guitars. They had alternatives. You look up to motivational speakers and art world professionals. You read Sun-Tzu and listen to rap music about drug dealing.

Someone says that love is autism for two and you “like” that and repeat it to others because it makes you feel less guilty about being alone. It makes you feel rational.

Oatmeal porridge being poured onto a red rose. Dreadlocks in a puddle of melting ice cream.

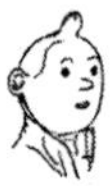

The way he argues is energizing. Then it's antagonizing. Then I don't want to listen. My face becomes mute and inexpressive. I'm staring through the table into infinity like I do in public transport.

He uses purple carrots so the Bolognese would be darker, more monochrome. I don't know how to eat the piece of Ox tail on my plate.

He is criticizing Kanye West as an artist. He is misreading what Kanye is. He is criticizing Kanye's scrappy go get 'em trendwhore attitude. Through Kanye he is criticizing the lower middle class and its undereducated nouveau riche appendixes. He doesn't know that he's doing that. He subliminally dislikes everyone who has to try hard, people who aren't born into wealth and/or cultural capital.

He's into sufficiently alt 15th century Flemish paintings and whatever the current smart white boy filter subgenre for popular music is. He believes that authenticity and high culture are not worn out markers of the past. He can already feel the dusty apathy of the position he argues from, but won't admit it, not yet.

The ease with which he mutilates other people's points of view is the main use he has for an outmoded classical education.

Pretty girls smile enigmatically and look down as he puffs his chest. Do they enjoy these displays of his lecturing intellect or do they feel embarrassed for him. Do they feel talked down to and is that a turn on or off?

He has a well-prepared entertaining rant about the uselessness of gender theory in art education. He dislikes feminist literature. Other people's bodies, orientations and traumas are uninteresting, he knows. He is already white and straight and has accepted what he looks like, so what's there left to talk about? He words it better.

Reading your friends' confessional poetry is pathetic, he says. You and all your friends are narcissists because you enjoy using Facebook, he says. He is always reading Shelley. He uses Facebook reluctantly. He embodies criticality on Facebook. He is not your average user.

He gets along well with older women who respond to his mid 20th century morals, his posh Bolognese and his measured heterosexual aggression.

He annoys me to no end. It's hard to figure out why. There's nothing unique about all of this. I feel like I want to fold inwards and fold and fold.

The way he talks about art is the way people who don't practice art talk about art. London is filled to the brim with discourse. There's no oxygen in the room.

He talks about how language is violent. It's like hitting someone in the head with a rock and talking about the inherent violence of stone. Words don't kill people, endless stern dad monologues do.

He annoys me because I recognise my tendencies in him. Caring more about winning the argument than about how the world is and how others experience it. He doesn't value experiences. He wants subscribers, not friends.

Failed communication. Blaming "the spectacle" or global capitalism for a sense of alienation that comes from feeling superior and being dead set on proving superiority.

I hate the way he uses analytical thinking as if it was a high tool. I see massive limitations in his "criticality". It acts as a filter between him and the expansive unreasonable beauty of the earth. He simply can't handle it.

He talks about moments without language, looking at a dog in the park, some kind of true experience. He doesn't understand what language is. He doesn't know ways to use it that don't require an escape or uses that coexist peacefully with an escape.

There is language that doesn't splatter worlds. Language that approaches Kanye from twenty different angles. Language that gently pokes and stimulates Kanye until he sources the traumas and ambitions that make up his God complex. To see Kanye not as an artist to criticize but as an illuminated image of the early 21st century. Someone to contemplate, to enjoy and to write egocentric feminist poetry about.

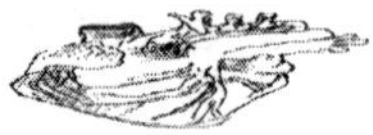

reality-house

three levels, several levels. different qualities, emphases base level, here's where most sexual acts happen. here we look like this there is no memory, or it is wiped every thirty seconds, people are like goldfish and never get bored

~base level~

BRAD is giving BORIS a blowjob.

BRAD (VOICEOVER): It's not like I don't have options. I know I do. You'll hear me talk about artists-as-brands and about making money and getting famous but it's not really that straightforward. Or I mean that's where I'm headed but I'm not propelled to it by desperate circumstances, although I am desperate but it's an internal sort of desperation. It's a drive I have that I don't know what to do with.

I came from middle class, my parents paid for schooling and I chose to use that support to pursue a career with little financial prospects. One could think that I was more idealistic then and that my idealism has left me since, but it's not really like that. Or it's true on a surface level but deep down I'd say that I always wanted to be in the art world because it's cut-throat and merciless. Competitive social spheres appeal to me. Everything else feels second rate. What I want to emphasize is that I did have a choice.

BORIS (VOICEOVER): I choose to believe that for him this is one of multiple options, his preference. I don't want to sense desperation or hesitation on his lips, on the tip of my cock. What I want to feel is his admiration, how he has read me and heard me talk and felt the weight of my opinion. He wants me in his mouth because he wants my strength, he wants to get closer, he wants to know more of me, intimate things. He can't have my insight, so he'll settle for my network.

BRAD swallows.

All well meaning advice that I get relates to how I should stop making work about the art world. I've taken this advice to heart. I've been advised to become less cynical and bitter or at least mask it better. The conversation reaches a sudden dead end when I say I'm not bitter or cynical at all. I'm a romantic, an optimist, an idealist, albeit a frustrated one.

Post Internet was a snappy definition for a poorly outlined macrotrend of artistic strategies that emerged in the mid to late 00's and coincided with an explosion of social media and microblogging platforms. Post Internet as a term was met with measured enthusiasm but also with immediate animosity and suspicion by those it was projected on. The artists who rode the trend the hardest were often the most vocal opponents of the term. Artists wanted singular and long lasting prospects, Post Internet was something brutal against that: it celebrated how similar we all were in the eyes of everyone even slightly removed

from the immediate core of the "scene".
Isn't it more authentic to be inauthentic than authentic if you're inauthentic at heart?
The cult of authenticity drives hipster culture.

Post Internet is the Marilyn Manson t-shirt you wear at 14 and are embarrassed by at 16 when you've moved on to Sartre and Einstürzende Neubauten. You wear black suit jackets and police other teens to become small adults too. That's what happened to most of us. We couldn't find the significant in the insignificant. We couldn't find the rave in our nu rave. Post Internet had its wings clipped when everyone became a post-minimal post-conceptual sculptor the art establishment could have a well-argued reasonable hard on for. Too bad the resources and old dude attention injected into these freshly emerged practices is also a kiss of death, although less wet and sloppy, less ultimate.

To be assimilated is to be forgotten. You find yourself alone in a room full of people. Because I love you I ask: don't hover above yourself. Who you are is better than who you want to be.

Agnes Varda made a great movie called "The Gleaners And I" about gleaning, the act of gathering remnants of crops from a field after the harvest. In the film Varda expands the definition, first to urban gleaners of trash and then to herself, a gleaner of images. I want to glean Post Internet, brush it off, form a layer of protection around it, see what it could still do. I want what no one else does.

Give me your twitter account, your personal brand,

Your huddled Tumblrs yearning to breathe free;

The wretched refuse of your teeming social media presence,

Send these, the homeless,

Tempest-tossed to me

I lift my lamp beside the golden door!

Sometimes I thought about leaving. When I felt undervalued. I thought about kissing him and did not go through with it. I had the power to disappear, to lessen him.

I knew he would be lonelier and would not be able to work as much. But I would lose too. I remembered what it was like: being alone and unremarkable. The thought of going back to that made me feel listless.

Dear Avant-garde,
The thought that you won't be in my life feels very difficult right now. I care about you more than I'd want you to know. I think, for you, knowing that would cause more anxiety.
I know you keep saying that it's not about me personally, that this is more general. On an emotional level I find it hard to grasp, sensing your fear and anxiety about being around me still hurts. It's fucked up to me how quickly you're giving up,

how accepting you are of this being how it is and how it has been and will be.

I mean that's true I guess, you'll push me away with measured success, this has happened to many other people I'm sure. This is where anger sets in, I want to disrupt your narrative, the one where you're pursued and expected to be this and that, needy emotional wells call for you to drown into them.

I'm adamant about proving to you that I can be indifferent as well, that this is something I've mastered, I can switch it on, or rather off. I guess what I'm saying is that I want to punish you, which is petty of me and not helpful.

My feelings are delayed. Something happens and there's a strange calm. Then it hits. I feel panicked so I'm writing this. I want to cry but I don't seem to be able to. It all feels a bit tasteless, and like you said: 'narcissistic and dramatic'.
all the best,
Jaakko

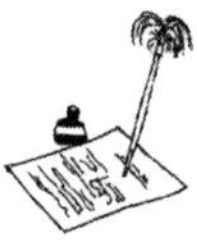

The artist has interests. She has an outlook, a position and a statement. The artist conducts research. She begins projects and completes them.

An installation is an assemblage of objects. The artist arranges the objects. The art is in the arrangement.

The artist attends social events relevant to her field. She enjoys herself and gains valuable professional contacts.

The artist speaks of the social and psychological world as if she did not speak of it.

The artist is humble. She refuses to succumb to greed and the envy that follows.

The artist is optimistic without being naive. Critical without being cynical. Attractive but not obvious. Reliable and not dull.

She has poise. Her self-esteem is evident in the way she carries herself.

The artist looks carefully at the objects/commodities around her.

She appropriates things. She picks up an object and examines it. She deems it interesting or uninteresting. She puts it back down. She does not compromise.

The artist works in the studio.
The studio is spacious, functional, ordered.
She receives guests: curators, journalists, fellow artists.
She has her routines.
In the mornings she cycles to the studio. She runs up the stairs. Her heart is racing.

She sits down. She drinks green tea.
Ideas are already half-formed.
Sometimes she acts upon them, sometimes she just sits there, perhaps noting something down.

I'm selfish with my time, she explains, she's smiling.
She feels free to refuse other engagements.
Her aim is to bore herself. Boredom leads to acts of creation.
She looks out of the window.

There are no curtains, the sun is shining in.

The space is raw.

I'm aware of my privilege and I'm grateful, she explains.

The artist has had social problems since early childhood. He is often alone when he does not want to be.

The artist makes vague gestures. What is realized does not amount to what he had hoped for. His life is not transformed in the process. He feels embarrassed. He feels listless.

The word mediocre comes to mind. It occurs to him that he might be that. Will the next forty years be a waste, he wonders. The artist makes plans to get out of art but realizes he is unemployable. He does not wish to be employed. Art begins as a refusal of culture. He has refused, arrived at a void, one that has not been filled or is only half full. It's me against the world and I do not suffice, he thinks.

To make art is to destroy the idea of art, he says.

The artist comes from middle class. He is slowly giving up on the hope of becoming middle class again.

It is viewed with second hand embarrassment and confusion. He's so weird, they say. To make an artwork is to destroy the idea of the work, he says.

The artist's earns below minimum wage. The artist is fallen middle class. He accepts money from his parents to appease them, and because he needs the money, because he doesn't want to learn how to do without it.

I don't want to think about money, all that bourgeoisie shit, the artist says. He says this often because he thinks of money often.

The artist does not eat meat. He is curiously torpid. The artist thinks he might have one chronic disease or the other. Is it depression or a liver disease that makes one not want to do anything?
It is summer and the artist hopes for darker curtains. The summer came too early and can't be dealt with, he says. The artist thinks about all the other artists who thought they would be great and ended up mediocre instead. There's nothing I can do to guarantee that won't happen, he says.

The artist makes something that's great. It all comes so easily to you, she says. I guess so, he says and smiles.

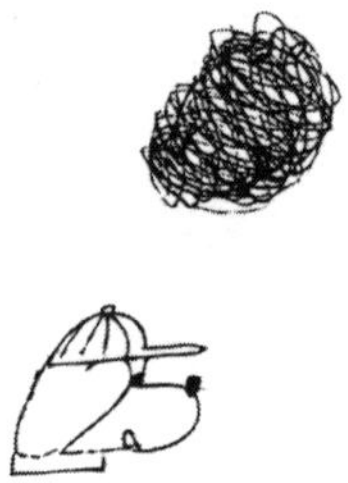

1.

The biological, historical, social and financial developments that enable the object.

2.

I'm deciding on a form without knowing what the content will be. I only know that I want the fabric and that I want to print on it, arduously and with high expense.

3.

Feeling sad made me feel powerless and feeling powerless made me feel vindictive. I wrote about the conflict in real time. He hurt my feelings and I didn't think about why, just marked down the how and the when: casually, just now.

4.

I wanted to print the resulting text on the fabric. I would exhibit it. Like Cruel Intentions: Sebastian's journal circulated at his funeral, Kathryn humiliated and defamed. Annette driving away in Sebastian's Jaguar with his journal at her side.

5.

I begin to think that I'm stronger than him. He is older and more defeated, more insecure, more not-together. Entropy, like time, runs in one direction only. Material objects wear out. The universe is cooling down.

6.

She talks about money. How to make it, what to make of it. I can be indifferent when we talk and feel weak and tempted later. I want to figure out how to manufacture stable objects that can be turned into cash. Moneyed, I wouldn't have to live with roommates and could cross continents at will (in order to see him or whoever). Life would be less tricky and stressful. I don't want to admit this. I don't want to have a scheme. I want to play the art game like I'm playing Monopoly. Exuberance matched by indifference. In hopes that I won't be a bitter loser and won't solidify successes or failures into a self-image. This has less to do with morals and more to do with sustainable growth. Raw ambition with little substance leads to dilapidation from the inside out. First the core goes, then there's incessant partying or exercise. Drug problems and eating disorders. There is broken glass everywhere.

7.

Possible DJ names:

DJ Social Benefits

DJ Every Fiber Of Your Being

DJ Cool

8.

animals sense danger in him and perhaps they sense accurately, he's something like an animal himself.

he's small and adolescent like in behavior and facial features. he's wearing big camouflage and i think frequent drug users always are. he sits down and bottles fall and break. there's broken glass everywhere. undercover cops bust a turkish drug dealer right next to the gallery. it's unusually cold for this time of the year, i'm shivering and looking on. the other guy with the bugged out eyes fucks with a fighter dog who is this close to biting his face off

9.

He is tired and jumpy. He is slouching in front of his computer.

ACT ONE

Reporter: The world is made up of levels. Like a high-rise or a video game. We are on LEVEL ONE. You can feel the gravitational pull. It's the year 1000 B.C.

Brad: I say something. Boris: I ask a question. How?

Brad: I elaborate.

Boris: When I listen to you, I listen for pauses to insert myself in.

Reporter: On LEVEL ONE the most ancient part of the brain dominates. The reptilian part. Chilled emotions and plain instinct. Bodies measure changes in temperature. You learn basic controls.

Brad: It's not like I don't have options. I know I do. You'll hear me talk about artists-as-brands and about making money and getting famous but it's not really that straightforward. Or I mean that's where I'm headed but I'm not propelled to it by desperate circumstances.

Boris: You're not?

Brad: I am desperate but it's an internal sort of desperation. It's a drive I have that I don't know what to do with.

Boris: Sounds like a misplaced survival instinct.

Reporter: The characters are laid back surfaces. Always the same. The acting is poor. The actors have learned to lie but are not good at it yet.

Brad: I'm middle class, my parents paid for schooling and I chose to use that support to pursue an art career, ostensibly with little financial prospects. I wanted to be in the art world because it's cut-throat and merciless. Competitive social spheres appeal to me. Everything else feels second rate. What I want to emphasize is that I did have a choice.

_:_:_:_:_:_

Reporter: The sex act is a catalyst, it makes things happen faster, it makes them intense. He wouldn't be curated into this or that without it. We are service providers until we grow and are ready to begin to receive.

Boris: I want to feel his admiration, how he has read me and heard me talk. He has felt the weight of my opinion, my cultural influence. He wants to suck me because he wants my strength, he wants to get closer, he wants to know more of me, intimate things. I don't want to sense hesitation at the tip. He must submit eagerly, but it should not be too easy for him.

ACT TWO

Reporter: LEVEL TWO is wish fulfillment for the people from LEVEL ONE. Here we talk about things. Bodies are discussed in a detached manner, as if they weren't in the room. Bodies are worked on so they would be more pleasing to look at. It's 2012 AD.

Boris and Brad are at a gym. There are men of different sizes and body types around them, pumping iron and skipping rope.

Boris: Did I mention that there are no women left? There are no great women artists. There's no one.

Brad: We tried to explain it with evolutionary psychology: some lack of height, ambition, testosterone.
Boris: Women existed to create new life and to create a domes-

ticity and we're full of life and there's too much of it already.
Brad: We're the last generation, the last billions.

Boris: The women, they just disappeared. We were surprised and shocked for a while and then carried on.

Brad: We touch screens, the screens don't feel like anything. I write things and take photos of things. I use the latest imaging software. The results are sent to printing facilities, somewhere, I don't know where. All art arrives in UPS boxes. I'm afraid to touch it. I don't want to damage it.

Boris: The work is handled with white cotton gloves by professionals.

Brad: What I'm saying is that I don't have a craft.

Boris: We are knowledge workers. When I feel alienated from my body I sip whiskey and light up. I'm not into conservation. My body will be cremated, the ashes scattered alongside other ashes. It helps that I had a childhood and a youth outside of data streams. I went fishing and rode my bicycle. Chopped wood, camped, all that.

Brad: Sometimes I think of myself as a sculptor. Instead of marble I'm sculpting myself. Through repetition I carve muscles. I focus on my abs. I'm making myself more fuckable, so lovely, a picture of health. I also sculpt public relations. Every like, tweet, hit, re-blog. Individual clicks are forming into a point cloud. The cloud is saying that people should pay attention to me and that they do.

Boris: I nod in agreement when you talk. I say “yeah, that’s interesting.” My eyes are glazing over, I’m thinking about something else. You are slowly arriving at points made a hundred times before, I’m politely waiting for you to get there. I’m interested in your interiority, not the mental kind. I’m interested in what your guts look like. I’m interested in penetration.

Brad: I’m talking and people feign interest in what I’m saying. This is one of my worst fears, that I’m seen but not heard exactly. They look at me and think about fucking me. What do I look like when I’m sleeping, they wonder. They imagine me drooling on a pillow.

Boris smokes a pipe.
Brad cuts his toenails.

ACT THREE
Brad writes into a journal with an 18th century quill. A candle burns.

Brad (voiceover): Our way of life came to an end quicker than we would have imagined. We joked and obsessed about the end and then it was there, fully-formed, irreversible. The end meant a dire lack of resources. We knew hunger. Living was about

survival again. It was all hardcore. We were being tested and I came out on top. There are only two of us left. I've dug into Boris. He's still alive.
He's a nutrient that keeps me company.

Brad moves towards a table with a white sheet over it, Brad draws the sheet out of the way and reveals a half-eaten Boris. Brad slaps Boris on the cheek, tenderly, to wake him up.

Brad sticks a spoon into Boris's open stomach. He eats guts.

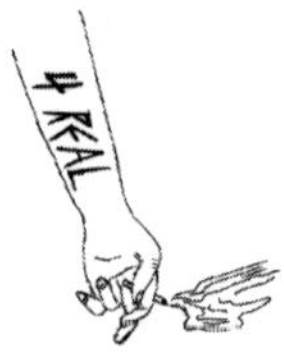
4 REAL

§

2013 was a year of discouraging information about the art system. I became more aware of, and more displeased with, the amount of affective labor involved. The pathetic leveraging of one's youth and cool (both more perceived than deeply felt). The fact that I somehow both surfed in on a #trend and missed my wave. One day you're in, the next day you're out. In an accelerated information age it really was a matter of days.

So I became interested in whatever else. Organized religion, peace, solitary sports, energy healing, socialism, love, tarot card readings, suburbs, drugs, planetary movements. Nothing stuck. I bought a flight to London. It was October.

§

JP: tried to go to wolfgang tillmans's house

for a party

or was told to go

and then didn't get in

and got the flu

lol

it was super depressing

or not really

like i skipped frieze opening

because i wanted to feel pure

but then i got dragged in2 this nonsense and it backfired in a humiliating way

shouldn't be this thirsty obvs

i wrote a 2500 word thing about it

and this quaker meeting that i went to

R: Oof. That doesnt sound fun. did u post it yet?
JP: i didn't

it's gonna be really good tho

i should write about berlin too

like how it "used to be"

R: At least you always make something productive

JP: that people would just go to a bar after the opening

R: Over your suffering

Your like jesus

JP: and now it's like half take a taxi to the private dinner

and half remain standing on the curb like lol what happened

private life / work life collapse

§

I went to a Quaker meeting with someone who I had met one week earlier who had mentioned his background and present affiliation with the movement. We had talked about the history of it, the exemplary track record Quakers had with defending civil rights, etc. freedoms. I had been interested in Quakerism since Nate's Quaker slut subplot during the last season of Six

Feet Under. I sent this person a pushy e-mail about going to one of the meetings. There was a meeting that conveniently overlapped with the Frieze opening. " I think everyone's at the PV for Frieze on the 16th but i'm not super interested in that so no matter. Yeah, so next wednesday maybe? ", I wrote and felt nonchalant and cool.

(Maybe in this non-hierarchical worship one could have a sense of belonging or a way to relate to people that wasn't 'productive' or profit- oriented. This felt novel in the context of the city.)

We went to the meeting. Then we had some dinner.

We had mediocre sushi and I had my teriyaki salmon and talked about how I had faked mental illness to get out of armed service and how that had taught me that I didn't have to do things that I didn't want to do, that systems were games that one could beat, that there were cheat codes and exceptions. To some other ears it would've sounded like I didn't have a sense of social responsibility, but I had surrounded myself with people who saw the absurdity of national interests and the absurdity of weaponized masculinity.

I felt very calm after the meeting. I was happy to have shared silence with those people and to have shook their hands. Happy to be talking around the experience while consuming this weak London-priced sushi. I felt like I had made the right decision not going to the Frieze opening. That it was a moral decision and a decision that carried a lot of symbolic weight. I liked that I had made it into a big deal and that I could feel accomplished merely by refusing to do an irrelevant thing that was easy to refuse.

§

Notes about the meeting:

-feeling dirty and messy walking to the meeting

-illegal alien with no spiritual passport because of atheist background, lack of inherited spiritual wealth

-sitting down in the back, kind of too close to people when there were empty seats more sparsely divided

-rushing thoughts, not making sense, thinkin about emails, thinking about if my thinking about these things was affecting the energy i was sending out and if it was bothering the other worshippers

-the man who stands up and sings a hymn

- the man who talks about being a good samaritan

- talking at the end of the meeting about peace activism, anti arms trade

§

After sushi we went to a bar. It was the birthday of someone I didn't know.

The bar was empty at first and then began to fill with people coming from Frieze. I had a flu and was not supposed to drink. I drank shots with tomato juice, chili, vodka and garlic because they sounded healthy.

We talked about what it's like to be bullied in school and if there was anything to learn from it.

A small group of people talked in hushed tones about continuing elsewhere. I overheard and they felt obliged to inform me: a party at Wolfgang Tillmans's house.

You should come, she said and I said Yeah.

My intuition was that I was too tired and frazzled and wanted to avoid social discomfort. But when they left I followed. Slowly towards a bus stop. Get cash on the way. We took some bus to an uneventful looking posh quiet neighbourhood.

We found the house. We found out that there were too many of us. Only one of us was really supposed to be there. You couldn't just bring your friends. It wasn't a 'studio party'. Ok let's just go, I said. Let's wait, he said.

One smart guy gave up immediately. I have to work anyways, he said and kissed her on the cheek and walked into the night. The rest of us stood behind the closed door.

We stood there for 10 minutes or so. They kept opening the door for people to leave. Then four or five people from our group decided to go for it and managed to walk in. The remaining three of us got stopped and shut down. We went back to standing outside looking confused, more acquaintances pulled up in taxis and insisted on getting in and did get in. I felt like I shouldn't get in and also didn't want to get in enough. I didn't look the part, I didn't feel the part, I felt like I didn't give a shit, merely wanted the ambivalence of the situation to come to an end.

I felt like an old person. I felt uncool which made me feel grounded and bright. I was like let's go but M had good reasons to try and get in. Her friends were there and not answering her calls. She had to stay out until 3.30 am and then take a flight. She wanted company and she wanted to say goodbye.

We decided to give it another chance. I told her maybe she should try on her own, that it was more likely that way. But we ended up trying together, the three of us. I smelled like yesterday's cigarettes and looked bloated. Uh oh, I thought.

We knocked on the door one more time. It was the same duo of apologetic, frustrated, teeth grinding thin assistants who were not used to bouncer work, weren't being paid enough for this shit. Then Tillmans himself walked up the stairs, holding a glass of wine and half a cigarette. He told us to leave in a polite, firm German manner. We finally got the message. He was still talking when I backed away and began walking towards the bus stop.

We walked away and were laughing a bit and I don't know, I laughed and it felt like it was really funny and I didn't give a fuck but I didn't want to be too happy about it because it might also feel like a real defeat and I didn't know how the others felt about it. I turn rejection into identity, energy and drive. I compared and contrasted with previous rejections. Affirmed outsider status is a fountain of youth.

It was not an exclusion from a group of peers which would have been serious, more an exclusion from a museum of past achievements and

current bottom-feeding.

§

The energy that drew people to the party: 1995 and Kate Moss and skinhead looking young gays, bleached denim, suspenders. Quaint nostalgia for comprehensible Gen X image production. A time when 'fine art photography' was a thing.

(Photocopies, analogue techniques, merging high and low and

using direct flash or whatever natural light is there. Some abstraction. And he is really good or that brand is really good, but the brand is also laid to rest in this glorified suburb. The exchange of ideas that can no longer be had. The price of market value is the death of content.)

§

I was not a person in their eyes. Just thirsty scum. Another nobody looking for ways to leech off the abilities of others.

§

This attempt at social climbing was in drastic contrast to the quaker meeting: breathing backs and coughs and churning stomachs no talking no personal brands no listed achievements no names on the doors no ways to be unique and good or ways to be those things but not moreso than others. Looking for light like photography never could.

M thought I saw something morally reprehensible or petty in people's behavior. The way the group split up. The way people ditched each other and fucked their 'communities' over to be able to access more VIP set-ups. I said that I didn't really mind. I was more surprised by my own boundless optimism than other people's thirst for elevated status, I said. Secretly I judged them.

I felt lazy and unwilling to attend tiresome openings and afterparties and gallery dinners because I did truly believe we were the future. That success would find us or meet us halfway at least. Or that there was no need to succeed in order to live. That Marxism or whatever consisted of defending the 'unsuccessful' majority's right to happiness. I sounded convincing and almost believed what I was saying.

§

The thirst and struggle London was fueled by had nothing to do with content, substance, intellectual projects, meaningful debate. I was only interested in things that I was interested in and these things did not include my financial future.

§

M said that I should see the power of my outsider position and I said that I could not claim to be an outsider. It was not a co-incidence that I was in London now, during 'Frieze week'. Not earlier or later. I was a conflicted person.

Later I thought about it from a different angle and realized that there was a confidence in me that related to this feeling of being outside in a deeper way. That no matter what connections I made or what I could 'achieve' through gaming the art system I would always feel disconnected from its core. That I could never truly buy into it, and that the Art World would always be turned off by the ambiguity of the Warez that I was selling. Was this a promise I was making to myself? Why was I so sure about it? Maybe it was the only way to think that allowed me to continue.

I thought again about the Quaker meeting and about how people seemed beautiful and dignified and a bit scary. Collective will and the search for a higher connection rendered people beautiful.

It was easy to construct this binary: people walking out of Tillmans's house, the cokehead gallerists and boyfriends of shithead former love interests, the stressed assistants; they weren't ugly by any means but they weren't glowing like the Quakers. Art hustlers were grey like the October that enveloped them. Not earth bound but not floating either. A frustrated middle. I always had to idealize one group while shitting on another.

§

(and M says yeah like you shouldn't read anything into this, nothing exceptional happened here and i'm like yeah that's true it's just funny because of the contrast to this whole quaker thing, that i set out to avoid the structure, to do something else, but then to remember about myself that oh yeah i am really thirsty and desperate too and falling flat on my face with that, like this rejection that i live for. like wanting it enough to appear as someone who wants it but not wanting it enough to get it, which will leave me in that awkward middle space where most people reside. so i don't feel alone at least. one day yr #trending the next day zero likes.)

§

Desperation and hope against all odds, despite all we knew

about neoliberal career games: that 99 out of a 100 would lose.

§

My ambition is not mine. It's what I'm a slave to. People get fooled into unpaid internships, dead end precarious art careers, student debt. The promise is that you are unique, you are worth it. You find out that some people are more unique than others. The economy has gone to shit and is only booming for 0.1%. The middle class will be a historical anomaly. London doesn't run on wages anymore. Cultural workers are not driven by consumption but by desire for some abstract idea of self-fulfillment and a sense of meaning. How to make people work 15 hours a day in the service of their 'personal brand' while they barely make rent. How to make them psychologize their failures quickly enough to not see a larger pattern here.

Everyone's in debt to the institutions that lied to them and made them self- critical in a paralyzing way (Goldsmiths, etc.). Most already know that it's a debt they will default on. The promise of self-fullfillment revealed itself to be a ponzi scheme.

§

JP: i'm not thinking about this because i think that i'm going to lose

necessarily

i'm thinking about this because collectively speaking 99 out of a 100 will lose

and those who will lose will include people that i love

and most likely me as well

and what's the point of winning if you win over your peers.

the only thing exceptional/noteworhty bout this rejection was how clear it was

usually art world rejection comes in a highly impersonal / institutional form the social rejetion is usually more implicit and even subtly encouraging

the hierarchy desires determined young sluts and will feed them crumbs to keep their hopes up

they don't want young hopefuls to lose interest because that would lead them to gravitate towards other engines of meaning production

the usual case is that the wolfgangs of the world don't want us to come in but don't want us to leave either

just want us exactly where we are, standing behind the door

clawing at it with our anemic limp wrists

it was refreshing to bluntly request something that you weren't supposed to have (access 2 this party) and to be denied it

it was refreshing to be told to fuck off
i felt really young

§

I woke up the day after the events and was ill. It was the standing outside, my stress level, poor eating and drinking, not taking care of myself. My throat hurt. I cancelled my plans and stayed in. I was browsing Tumblr from my bed and then fell asleep.

I had a dream where I was sitting on a white sofa. There was a glass coffee table in front of me. A complex white rug under it. My macbook was on the coffee table. It had its lid closed.

Wolfgang Tillmans walked into the room. He sat next to me. He took my laptop and looked at it without opening it. Which constellation is that? he asked. I looked closer and noticed that there were small dots of light, like stars, shining trough the outer shell of the computer. I don't know, I said. I think it's Libra, he said.

Metaphorically, Libra the Scales serves as an age-old symbol of divine justice, harmony and balance.

Libra is the only zodiac sign that does not symbolize a living creature.

Works

1. Letter

I wrote a letter and hid it in the studio building. I told people about the letter.

2. Portrait

I observed someone's gestures from a distance and made detailed notes.

3. White Flag

I tied a mosquito net to a severed tree branch.

4. Choice

I broke a branch into three parts and worked on one of them.

5. Drawing

I burned an X on a piece of wood using sunlight and a magnifying glass.

6. The Acknowledgement That This Is Boring Doesn't Make It Any Less Boring

I asked someone to stand still and hold a sign saying I KNOW THIS IS BORING for one minute.

7. Funeral Confetti

I cut VHS tape into small pieces. I scattered the pieces on the floor.

8. The Room

a) I removed the surface material from a part of a wall to make bricks visible.
b) I arranged objects (mosquito net, two tree branches, two metallic table frames, four pieces of rope) to make a division in the room.
c) I cleaned the floor but did not do it well.
d) I placed a small piece of paper on a spiderweb and later removed it.

e) I asked someone to enter the room and casually drink the water from a plastic cup placed on the floor.

Research (A Letter From Camp)

1.

a) I don't know how much I want you to know.

b) I want you to know that I don't care.

2.

3. She assumes that I'm lazy. I'm looking at her glasses.

a) It's all up to you.

b) You need to push yourself.

c) Use that feeling.

4.

5. I listen to her talk about her work. I nod. That's nice, I say.

6.

a) I walk around the building aimlessly. People are touching video cameras and organic materials.

b) In July in Berlin there was a blackout. People in the building opposite brought candles to their balconies and sat there reading or talking or looking at photographs. I stared at them for some time. Later, I saw some people fucking in the living room of one of the first floor apartments. You couldn't see much, a pale back hovering over a leather couch.

7.

a) I want people to see the room without forming an opinion about it. b) I want to point out that it's interesting.

8.

The room has two doors and one window. One door leads to the hallway, the other door to a similar room on the right. The window has metal bars. The room is on the ground floor. The floorboards are arranged in a diagonal pattern. There are hooks and cables and former lamps and electrical sockets. There are spiderwebs in the corners. There is a lot of other stuff.

9.

– I really like your breathing room.

– I can't take credit for how the wind moves.

10. The room and the objects placed there are not the work. The text is not the work. The drawings are not the work. You're not going to see them.

11.

a) I fall asleep at lectures, at my desk, on a rug, in an armchair, in another kind of chair, on the floor.

b) People take pictures of me while I sleep.

c) During the night I grind my teeth and have nightmares. 12. Things should be cool.

13. I try to draw him without him noticing. He notices.

14. I'm holding the string, I'm not sure the timing is right. We pull the string, it cuts into the skin on my right index finger. The chair moves, a beer bottle has been placed on it and falls.

15. I'm extremely similar to another person.

16.

17. There's a camera filming her filming them. The other cameras are in the crowd, in a tree, behind the hill, attached to her, in his face. I'm filming from a distance. I make sure I'm not visible in any of the footage.

18. We got swing dancing.

19.

a) They're looking at the drawing while I'm drawing it.

b) How long will it take for you to recognize my brilliance?

20.

a) A dragonfly is flying around, it keeps touching the 80's floor material.

b) A laser printer is resting on an oriental rug.

21.

a) I'm in the secret room trying to make a calculated gesture. I become aggressive.

I empty a bottle of ink on the wall. I sweep the ink around with my hand, some of it goes into an open wound. I neatly hang a red curtain.

b) None of it made sense.

c) I see the red curtain in the hallway. Someone has removed it.

22. Some voices over others.

23. She's crying. I try my best not to look at her. I have an mp3 player. The same song is playing over and over again but I don't care to change it.

24.

a) I feel guilty for every passive-aggressive sigh and awkward expression.

b) This is not effortless or natural.

25. Style is the underlying purpose of everything.

26.

a) Are you freaking out, he asks. I say yes, he asks why and I reply something but I immediately forget what it was that I said.

b) I announce that I'm leaving. c) This is not my private conflict.

27. He's sitting in the armchair, he's staring at the wall and toying with the frisbee absent-mindedly.

28. I've only had time to complain.

29. A monumental glass fiber fountain is in the room. A view of a computer desktop is projected on it. The water is flowing. Photo Booth is open and I can see myself on the water. I'm smiling.

30.

31

32.
a) . I debate for hours over the placement and meaning of a found object. In the hospital 50 meters away people are learning how to walk again.
b) I'm afraid of being pretentious so I'll just not say it.

33. I'm trying to draw the lake, I don't want to swim. The sun is setting. I feel uncomfortable. On the way home I can't think of anything.

34.

35.

a) People talk about other people hooking up.

b) He announces that he is 100% straight. I didn't know desire could be so static and exact.

c) Most everyone agrees that the refusal of desire is sovereign: "I don't want to, that's all!" A white-collar bourgeois or an immigrant worker will tell you the same thing. And the left-wing student will repeat it even louder, for he has made desire sacred intellectually. As for me, when I hear someone express non-desire, I hear something behind it that could be: "Don't insist! Capitalism has inscribed this refusal in my body. "

d) On Saturday I spend hours in public transport to end up at an opening. American men wearing childish baseball caps. One of them has a really interesting nose. The work exhibited is a 74 minute fake Godard movie. In the first room a plastic alligator is holding a painting in its mouth. I'm amused for 30 seconds and then begin missing the point.

e) 1968 parodies.

36. I dance around the fire. It comes as a surprise to others that I'm able to do so.

I started thinking about what she had felt like when writing her comment, if her back was hurting, if she was sitting in a low-grade unergonomic chair.

Or maybe the chair was ergonomic and it was the monotony of her daily routine that made her back ache.

For some reason I started imagining that she had a boyfriend called Chad who was a grown up bro. They were having trouble in their relationship. They were taking a time-out. That's how 'dude' had slipped into her writing and why she was using my first name in a clash with critique tradition or whatever.

Maybe Chad had told her that all of his friends thought that she was 'stuck up' and 'no fun to be around' and now she was stressed about appearing more relaxed. She knew she had to conjure up a sufficient response to being more like 'one of the guys'. Can one be 'fun' and be an art critic at the same time? She hated this influence Chad had over her. She knew she was alright but it was hard not to take his critique to heart.

She was genuinely tired of the intellectual posturing of the guys in her class/ seminar/workplace. She didn't want to do that. Instead she wanted to speak a plain, well-read truth. She was real, she thought to herself. She felt like she had the license to be aggressive but it just didn't feel right. She wanted to find a way of speaking that would steer her away from direct conflict and more in this direction where whatever she said would kind of deflate these 'intellectuals', their posturing would shrink along with their argument. She would do this in an off-hand manner. She google image searched Dorothy Parker.

I thought about what she thought of me, how she interpreted the tone. How she thought that I was championing for an absolute beauty while I was pointing at this huge canyon between aspiration and reality.

I imagined her imagining me as slightly overweight and with a tan.. my teeth were glowing and white. I was confident and had good posture. I had been 'good at school'. I was socially aggressive, but in her imagined version I created more consensus than in real life. She assumed I was straight for no reason at all.

She had always been told that she had a good eye. She could tell that I wasn't the best at painting, like I had irresponsibly claimed. She could trust her eye to tell the difference, to inform her that these other artists I had mentioned were actually much better: that there was an absolute scale. But this was something that she wanted to imply rather than have a conversation about. It wasn't cool to talk about taste or subjective experience.

Her 2014 was about research and about 'issues'. Art had to make itself useful and be less obnoxious and elitist. She thought about the anxiety Chad and her parents felt in art galleries. How bad she felt when she wanted to involve them in her world and couldn't. She disliked snobbery and the mystery art had conjured up around itself. She sought to demystify and didacticize, even if there would be nothing left afterwards.

Artists in provincial towns self-medicate against depression, boredom and anxiety. They're slowly coming to terms with the fact that nothing they do will be seen, that none of it mattered.

His face is framed there. Minimal changes in expression but he's holding up pretty well. I keep the camera running so that the situation would become more uncomfortable. So he would have to reveal something. It doesn't get that uncomfortable.

My social alibi is paper thin. I say I'm a video artist when I need to record something or someone. I claim ownership. I'm fooling all of the people all of the time.

His face has been of interest for a few years. It doesn't matter if he is interesting or not. The face is one angle to the head. The head is sculptural: weighty and fragile. 'The ceramic head', we used to call him.

Recent desperate, socially destructive acts have put him over the threshold. I can think of him as a subject. He might be an actual person.

He was already drunk when he called me fat. It was one in the afternoon, I had walked back into the room. I know I am, I replied. He didn't know what he had done. I had been at war with my body for years.

He was set to perform. Wellbeing From Music, the performance was titled.

Sometimes he was singing. He drank more. I fell asleep in a corner of the room. A lot of stuff happened that day, I've scribbled down the details. The notes are a distraction. I have to focus. What I wanted to talk about was empathy.

In the middle of the performance I throw a glass of water in his face. He doesn't believe it, he gets up, I wish I could hit you right now, he says. He asks me if I've ever been in a fight. He doesn't wait for an answer. He assumes that I have not. You can hit me if you want, I tell him. He doesn't. Hold your hand like this, he demands. He slaps me in the palm, it's stings like an enthusiastic high five.

I feel like I should explain myself to him. I thought the performance needed a dramatic turn, I say. He had been mumbling for forty minutes, finishing his wine, being politely looked at and ignored. I felt like you wanted someone to stop you, I tell him.

Diamonds

February in Berlin is grey slush, concrete blocking the horizon, homeless teens looking for cheap amphetamine. Lazy expats with clouds of smoke for breath. Then it's Helsinki at its whitest and sharpest. All pure and unforgiving. The sun has come out again but the sea is still frozen. I walk on the ice and the sun radiates mania. I wake up at nine even if I went to sleep at 4 in the morning.

Diamonds

A random night in a cellar turned dance floor. I was angry at him and dancing furiously, pretending he wasn't there. He came up to me and tried to hug me. I turned my head away and held my arms stiff against my sides. He hugged me anyways, in my plank-like state. Then he left.

Diamonds

To love someone is to isolate him from the world, wipe out every trace of him, dispossess him of his shadow, drag him into a murderous future. It is to circle around the other like a dead star and absorb him into a black light.

Diamonds
What is love, baby don't hurt me, don't hurt me, no more

Diamonds
A certified, high-quality diamond created from a lock of hair or the cremated ashes of your loved one as a memorial to their unique life. A way to embrace your loved one's memory day by day. The most beautiful cremation jewelry keepsake available for honoring their unique life. Comfort and support when and where you need it.

Diamonds
I'll sharpen my quill and dip it in ink, I'll scribble something down and wrap it around the leg of my carrier pigeon.

Diamonds
Our last chat together. 26th of November 2012. 01:22 am
yeah, it's a tough nut to crack
how to engage in cultural production
without some trite sense of solidarity
or alternatively a black vortex of self-interest

Diamonds

Under other, more mundane feelings is the love I have for him which doesn't have a reason or a proper context. Love frightens me because it messes with the scale of things and makes me behave like an idiot. He's eating a burrito and I'm using my phone to make a video of it.

Diamonds

Rihanna tells me to shine bright like a diamond, or I hear her say that, it's not to me specifically. I want to tell her that diamonds don't shine, they reflect. And there's no reflecting bright. The brightness is dependent on the light source, not the diamond. Douglas Coupland writes some random shit about the diamond generation, overachievers
younger than me. I wish I was like them, pale and sharp. Unbreakable, reflective.

Diamonds

are forever. To have a diamond as a best friend. To be iced out. Maybe my heart is not broken after all. It's pulsing along and I'm keeping the beat. I see my reflection in the mirror behind the DJ booth and I see that I look cute and arrogant. I pout my lips like a duck. I'm sweating.

Diamonds

He is playing games with me. There are multiple games and the rules are unclear to both of us. My aim is truer than his. I think he wants to keep me at bay and keep my adoration at the same time. He is giving me enough rope to hang myself with. I feel foolish and very young when I realize he has outplayed me. This happens more than once. I listen to sad music as I walk home from the bar where he has crushed me again.

Diamonds

A memory of his drunk breath on my lips and his lips against mine and the realization that his lips don't physically exist anymore. How do lips rot? Lips embalmed, lips burning and becoming ashes.

Diamonds

To the elements it came from Everything will return.
Our bodies to earth,
Our blood to water,
Heat to fire,
Breath to air.

In his History of Western Philosophy, Bertrand Russell quotes an unnamed poet on the subject – "Great Empedocles, that ardent soul, Leapt into Etna,nand was roasted whole."

Diamonds

Let yesterday arrange itself around you in flat schematic images.

Diamonds

The first sunny day in recent memory. Walking on a frozen slice of the sea. It is firm ground for now. Ice fishing in the background. Men luring fish to the surface, to their deaths. The ice will crack and make an attempt to float somewhere else. It will melt instead. It's been two months since he passed away.

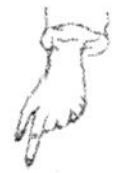

Everyone wants to understand art. Why not try to understand the song of a bird?
– Picasso

I feel angry and resentful at myself. I stop and calm down and try to comprehend: How did I become so enamored with the 'art system'? How did art become a desk job without stability or vacation days? Why am I burning out at 27? Why am I so god-damn thirsty?

Duchamp wanted to introduce time, a linearity, into a static craft. In a hundred years, a bland 'contemporaneity' followed. 'Researching' your 'projects', developing, hoping you were steadily improving while EasyJet flew you to homogenized biennials and you spewed CO_2 along with the planes. Inhale, exhale.
Maybe it was an accident. Accelerated doom. You get your

BFA, your MFA, your PhD. Papers you can't afford (9000£ a year). You get to know everyone. You upgrade on production value. Sometimes you despair: is there anything you can accomplish? You feel utterly alone. 33 notes.

When you think that something is about to begin it's probably peaking. There is no linear development in art. It's cyclical, wavy. Post Internet was at its best when we were waiting for it to start already.

Art is like farming or doing laundry. You do it and then you get to do it again. It's like oxygen. It's invisible and it envelops you. It doesn't get any better or worse than right now. Don't worry about it.

Success and failure are both a distraction. I want to let them go. I want to live on an island in Finland and make ceramics and felted hats. I want to be one of those unimpressive regular people you ignore on your way to the club. I'll be slightly overweight and wearing overalls. I'll be grounded and smiling while you ignore me.

I realize that I've been an extremist.

Duchamp switched art for chess, an infinite game where you can win individual battles but never the war. Art can be a game, by which I mean that it's an elaborate coreography with elements of choice and varied outcomes. It's a thrill. It's not your life.

I'm playing Candy Crush and Zen Bound 2 and 2048. Succeeding in these mobile puzzlers feels kind of like being curated into your awesome non- compensated group show in Seoul or Vienna or Oslo. Gaming comes without the distress, without being addressed, without coolness, without affect, outlook or statement.

2.

I watch Game of Thrones while drawing in my book. The drawings are something to do. They keep the anxiety at bay. They fool me into thinking I'm being productive when I can't get over the idea that I have to be productive all the time.

I don't exhibit the drawings because they're so pure and so emo. When I show them to people I regret it later on. I don't want to charge them with expectations, with the burden of communication.

It's a bad habit: you take everything you've got, your failures and insecurities. You repurpose, repackage, relaunch and repeat until they are categorized as successes. Experience is what you get when you don't get what you want.

Watching these Mortal Kombat gameplay videos. Mortal Kombat 9: All Fatalities on Shao Kahn HD. The word Success blinks on top of these carnivalistic, brutal executions. It's not enough to merely defeat your opponent; you must obliterate and make it funny, distinct, memorable.

Bullies have lower infection rates as adults than those who have been bullied.

Your life is like Gossip Girl except everyone is old and poor.

This is a placeholder for astute observations about capitalism, gender, precarity and 'post-digital' culture. I zoom out to reveal how my personal woes and struggles connect to a network. How political this is. How these

exact details communicate a universally human experience.
A picture of a Dutch painting. Bosch or Bruegel. A gettyimages tag. A wave filter. The bright blue of a projector with no signal.

Fatigue Fatigue

An article titled Network Fatigue was first published in Issue 16 of Frieze d/e. Written by Pablo Larios, the text focuses on the artistic significance of his mainly Swiss and American (Berlin-based) friend group.

I had a problem with the text and status updated about it on Facebook. I scribbled down some notes and chatted about it. No one wanted to comment on it in a public way. I felt the desire to do so and committed to writing a response. I'm having trouble remembering what the problem was. I'm re-reading the text and I'm like hmm. It's still annoying but it also seems like fairly harmless self-promotion.

I've been tired. I haven't been reading much art journalism. I went horseback riding and sailing last week (I don't really know how to do either). I'm interested in moving in ways that are complex and unnecessary. I'm interested in having these experiences. I don't know why I'm writing about myself here. Is this network fatigue? Or is this a breach of the kind of tact and exclusion expected of someone sufficiently fatigued and networked? Are my meals simple enough to be written about in Frieze?

Network Fatigue is a great title. The article sets out to describe something I think I ought to relate to. It seeks to brand tiredness, failure, withdrawal, but in an uplifting, twee way. Beginning with how the Internet rendered images worthless. Ending up somewhere that feels like home, but operates like a career.

The article mentions Calla Henkel and Max Pitegoff, Tobias Madison, Carissa Rodriguez, Emmanuel Rossetti. Highly image-conscious young artists operating in central geographical and virtual locations. They are framed through terms like ephemeral, local, personal. It reminds me of texts about saints and musicians, I'm waiting for Larios to go for 'humble' or 'down-to-earth'. That wouldn't happen, but would be funny if it did.

Jaakko: i was reading this 1994 chloe sevigny article that connects to this really well

Jaakko: where she's like still really alt and unknown and shopping at thrift stores but then also new yorker is writing about her and she's in a sonic youth video

Jaakko: like this weird tension between being thirsty for alt mainstream validation while wanting to have like a small special scene or whatev

Jaakko: maybe the argument can be that

network fatigue = grunge

tobias madison is eddie vedder

haha

i actually dont know what tobias madison is like at all

maybe he's more like a frank black or smthng

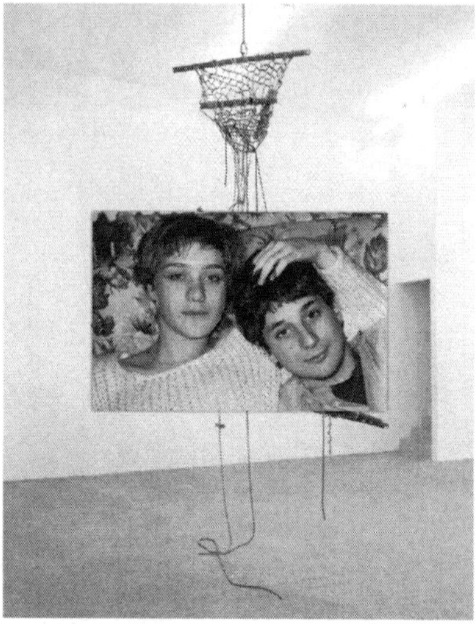

[image: Tobias Madison @ Kunstverein Munich overlaid with Chloe Sevigny & Harmony Korine on a sofa in the mid '90s]

Larios reports: The JPEG threatens to level the artwork into a flat, ethereal data-stream, while paradoxes like documentation preceding physical exhibition come to seem benign. Sleekness is commonplace, almost accidental. HD is unremarkable and on every storefront.

His ephemeral, local, cool, exclusive friendships are presented as an alternative to devalued overshared imagery: Madison submitted a series of dark, unfocused party photos to the blog Contemporary Art Daily following a request for images of Madison's show. Published online, the gesture wrested power away from the expectations of glossy, well-lit images for remote online viewing and back to the local, imperfect and temporary. The flip side to this – flip in both senses – might be that publicized intimacy is itself a way of fostering cult value: a gesture toward implied or real exclusivity.

I'm thinking of people I know who have no clue what Contemporary Art Daily is. I'm thinking: maybe submitting his blurry party photos to CAD is just Madison being good at his job? How are savvy PR strategies the closest thing we have to subversion? I guess Larios is asking the same question. Asking it does not suffice.

I assume that there is an art world, but maybe that's not the case. Maybe Larios is depicting the new status quo, a medieval landscape of villages and city-states, people loyal only to those in their immediate vicinity, having dropped any pretense of global consciousness. Would that be so bad? Maybe not.

Jaakko: twee obscures citizenship, adulthood, responsibility for self

twee idolizes quiet docile heteronormative bicycle-riding picnic blanket life

A bitter Dave Hickey would say: the party is now the art. Larios re-iterates the point, but with optimism. It's not the kind of party you're thinking of: a cocaine-fuelled rager at Miami Art Basel. It's not excessive or gross. The party is a slumber party between Larios and friends. It's a tasteful dinner you're not invited to. A wooden table painted white, legs uneven. Candles.

Agreeable, pretty, European friends chewing with their mouths closed. A full-bodied, pepper-y Syrah.

Elephant92: the comeback of the embodied image

Jaakko: soudns like a good twist

Elephant92: im tired of talking about how everything is glossy

and hd is life

Jaakko: yeah it's boring

so banal uuugh

Elephant92: it's not at all banal

that beheading video is not banal, sry

it's fucking terrifying
Jaakko: not gonna watch

Elephant92: it's scripted reality that is way more artful than ryan trecartin

Jaakko: i should include that

that images are not banal

and it's banal to say that images are banal

and it's a boring excuse for this twee slumber party scene

to pin it on this assumed 'banality'

altho i guess pablo is talking more about artworks than all images

Elephant92: twee slumber party also includes a lot of MDMA and fucking tho

Jaakko: i guess it's twee in the same way that Girls is

like it still has sadomasochism and like tattoos

Elephant92: maybe yeah

Jaakko: but the emotional aura is still twee
i really like the twee angle, gonna keep forcing it even if it's really unfair

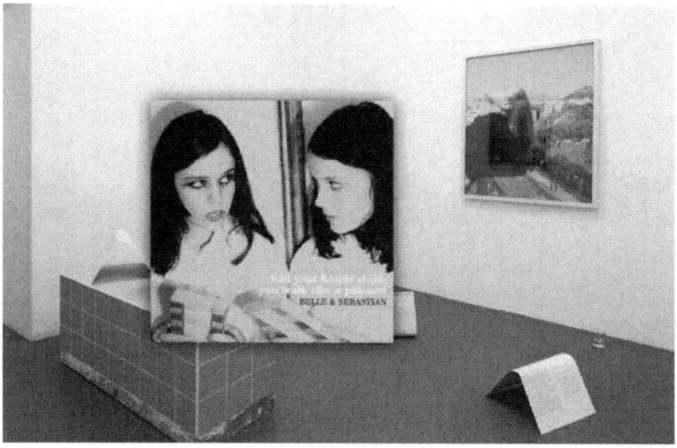

[image: Calla Henkel & Max Pitegoff @ T293, Belle & Sebastian album cover]

It was rainy in Istanbul. I walked up a steep hill, panting. I was out of shape and had a flu. I sat on the couch in the office and closed my eyes. I crossed my arms behind my head and took slow breaths.

Tobias Madison walked in with his crew. He had just arrived from LA. He was not an Eddie Vedder. He was his own person. He had a friendly smile. He was serving graphic-designer-from-Stockholm realness. He shook hands with everyone and introduced himself. Oh, you Facebook messaged me, he said. Yes, I said.

We were in the same residency by coincidence. I guess neither of us was thoroughly network fatigued. I had contacted him before his arrival to ask him if he wanted to talk to me about my potential response to the article.

He went to the balcony to puff on his e-cigarette. I joined him and a group of others there. The sky was gray. He wore a chain around his neck. On the chain a 1:1 human nose cast in silver. I looked at it and tried to figure out if it was a cast of his nose. It didn't occur to me to ask.

We had a long conversation about the article. I didn't record it. I didn't take notes. I wasn't feeling like a journalist. My shaky recollections would do. I typed some stuff into my phone.

He said he didn't try to belong anywhere and I thought that I always tried and that was probably behind feeling excluded, the trying.

He used the word 'defend' in relation to the article. Larios was defending a certain mode of artistic production. What was this mode being defended against? Madison made a point about gender, that maybe the article was about gender. Maybe these elusive, ephemeral, wistful, whispered strategies were a stance against a certain type of art world machismo, of space-taking. Confident bros had eclipsed the rest of us, was it a way to resist them, to be invisible?

Madison talked about 'equalized space' in terms of Times and New Theater, the spaces in Berlin run by Henkel & Pitegoff. I thought it was an interesting term. It made me think of well-mixed music. Was equalizing a kind of flattening? I thought of those spaces as 'cool', and that as cool spaces they excluded certain elements, most elements. Were coolness and equality compatible? I was asking too many rhetoricals but didn't want to stop.

Madison's position was hard to pin down. I approached the conversation as a debate. I tried to articulate a clear position that could be agreed or disagreed with. Somehow he managed to stay opaque and ambiguous. He had a cat-like languor. Maybe this was network fatigue: network dreaminess, network indolence, network diplomacy.

I perceived hard choices where he perceived none. I felt crass for trying to push resolutions. I asked him if he considered submitting the blurry party photos to Contemporary Art Daily a subversion, and what he thought the difference was between submitting them and simply not submitting anything.

He asked me why I cared about the article, why did it feel like I needed to react to it. I think he used the word 'attack' here. I said I was interested in it in relation to a recent history of authenticity. The history of youth. I talked about Chloe Sevigny a bit.

Lunch was served. Street cats visited the office like they tended to do in Istanbul. Tobias Madison let one of the cats sit in his lap. Tobias Madison fed the cat a piece of potato from a stew. The piece was balanced on top of a radiator, the cat pushed it down to the floor. A splash of orange stew on the radiator to mark the event. The cat played with the potato before consuming it.

Talking to Madison helped me understand the (not-so-)subtle shade in the article (or: he put me on the wrong track). That it was written in opposition to conflict-driven high visibility singular practice boy geniuses that had dominated Berlin art terrain for a few years. It was probably about Simon Denny, Timur Si-Qin, Daniel Keller, Oliver Laric, etc. I assumed that Madison and Larios and all young people with taste were now against the idea of "Post Internet" in general and of male, sculptural Post Internet in particular.

Larios had alluded to his distaste in previous writing. In his review of 'Speculations on Anonymous Materials' (Post Internet-y group show at Fridericianum in Kassel, Spring 2014) he had written: During the night of the opening, three of the exhibiting artists began to quarrel and were asked by guests who preferred to enjoy their dinners to take their argument elsewhere. Anyone who peeked over a balcony could witness a curious zoological display: a trio arguing various 'positions' on materialism, biological determinism, machismo. Regardless of the sides being argued, the real takeaway here was unfortunate. Everyone lost, because the playing board was already faulty. Just as enlightenment once to led to barbarism, now theory leads to dogma, and dogma leads back to unenlightened conflict – now in HD.

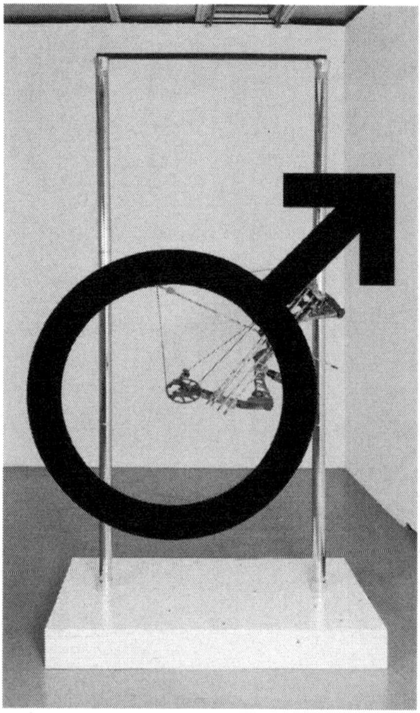

[image: Timur Si-Qin, 'Bow on stripper poles', 2012, overlaid with Mars Symbol]

I feel like the Network Fatigue article would've worked better if it had gone for blood. If Frieze d/e is mainly a forum for hashing out local art world politics, that could've happened in a transparent, juicy, reality-as-in-reality-TV way. The article should've pointed to the masc art game itself as *the* source of fatigue, instead of scapegoating innocent 'banal' images. Image circulation online is an escape for gender dysphorics and autists and lonely teens worldwide. The internet has saved thousands, if not millions, of queer lives. Then again, I guess the talk was of artworks, not lives. Although, in Network Fatigue, I'm not sure what the difference is.

Afterword

'Scorched earth' is a military tactic of utter devastation and a video game, and now it's a book of selected writings by Finnish artist Jaakko Pallasvuo. Scorched Earth is made up of texts that Jaakko wrote between summer 2010 and September 2014. He posted them on his tumblr DawsonsCreek.info alongside images of new works that he'd made and announcements for shows he was in and drawings and other stuff like that. Dawson's Creek was the name of US TV show from the late '90s and early 2000s. It was about a white suburban teen named Dawson Leery, a close group of his friends, and the drama of their high school lives. I was 11 when it first aired and found it unbearably sappy.

Tumblr is a microblogging platform and social networking site known as a safe haven for angsty teens looking to express themselves through rants and GIFs. Jaakko really opened up about his life and his thoughts about art in the writings he posted there. He conveyed a real sense of sincerity despite that affected online world. In the end, through his openness, he might have an impact on what he's known for. I hope he does, because I respect the way he went about it, and because that's one of the powers that artists' writings apparently have. Some artists write seemingly impenetrable mystifications of their work. And some writers do that for them. But some pretty great artists have invested time and energy into informing the discourse around their work, demystifying its origins and its meaning while making an argument about how it should make its way into history—Robert Smithson, Adrian Piper, Dan Graham, Mike Kelley, Renée Green, John Miller, Jutta Koether, etc., etc. I wanted to mention these names in relation to this book at least once, whether you agree with the association or not.

Jaakko makes it pretty clear which artistic and social context he wants his work to be seen in relation to: "I want to glean Post Internet, brush it off, form a layer of protection around it, see what it could still do. I want what no one else does." He wrote this while passing through an art scene in Berlin and London that wasn't sure how it felt about the label—which Jaakko calls "a snappy definition for a poorly outlined macrotrend of artistic strategies that emerged in the mid to late 00s and coincided with an explosion of social media and microblogging platforms." In the meantime, the label has come to more or less stick, because there's a bunch of artists and writers and gallerists and curators and probably collectors who decided they could get something out of it. Still, to an extent, just as it was when Jaakko wrote the words back in March 2013, "Post Internet is the Marilyn Manson t-shirt you wear at 14 and are embarrassed by at 16 when you've moved on to Sartre and Einstürzende Neubauten. You wear black suit jackets and police other teens to become small adults too."

Speaking of, there's this great review of Marilyn Manson's 2012 album Born Villain, written by the artist Morag Keil, in the Autumn/Winter 2012/2013 issue of the artist-run magazine Provence. In it, she argues that, early on, "Marilyn Manson made himself into a brand and then we bought it." And that with the new album, Manson "has not taken off the mask but created a third position between the product and the person." It's exactly these negotiations regarding the 'artist-as-brand' that we find everywhere in the contemporary art world that Jaakko writes from.

The thing is, though, that Jaakko's writing outlines a strategy significantly different than the one most others have gotten to work for them. While lots of people have been putting up streamlined products for sale, including efficiently aggregated and affected subjectivities that can stand to take on just about any look, behavior, or criticism thrown at them, Jaakko has been dealing semi-publicly with those parts of himself that it's often inconvenient to let show in social situations. That flies in the face of this contemporary art world, where social and professional interactions constantly veer toward some grisly hybrid—where most people meet the restrictions on participation with euphoric acceptance.

But Jaakko's world is something we can as good as see through his eyes, given the imagery he erects to describe objects and affects familiar to most of today's readers. He can script a hypothetical scenario—don't forget, we're talking about a sometime video-maker—with as much style as the similarly scripted chapters of Bruce Hainley's recent Sturtevant book. And he peppers us with language that's real enough to stick to the roof of your mouth: beard stubble and a list of potential DJ names and profit-oriented personal relationships and sushi and back pain and ergonomic furniture and February in Berlin and dance floors and BFAs/MFAs/PhDs and Canon DSLRs and body image issues and pure information and internships and debt. Time and again, his subjects are punishingly real and banal: "You're on a double decker bus, it's raining, you haven't eaten properly and have a headache."

Between boldfaced reflections on his life and work in art, we get solemn vignettes of a kind of Romantic future, images and situations often without sufficient context, character sketches of artist types and art making strategies. We get "He" and "She" whereas most of the world thrives on name recognition. As a result, we're reminded that something could be at stake here, and we're left feeling more or less alone with Jaakko. "Do you think of people as material?"—he asks someone he's filming for a video he's making, someone smoking a hand-rolled cigarette between beetroot-stained fingers. That line's a whole lot like one from Ben Lerner's 2011 debut novel *Leaving the Atocha Station*: "My look accused them of [...] treating people and the relations between people like things." In fact, Pallasvuo and Lerner's Atocha have a couple things in common: that language of a banal reality that sticks to the roof of your mouth, and struggles with the thought of being a failure, and for it, a fraud.

At times writing from his home country of Finland, Jaakko sets a geographic outside on the same plane as social exclusion and body-consciousness. He gives middle-class straight white weaponized macho male normativity names like "Brad" and "Chad" and "Boris" and then picks at those parts of it that relate to him as well. He gives penetrating insight into what's being leveraged, what a statement or act always also means. He writes like he's giving words to all the unspoken motivations that actors try to convey with their eyes, through their silence, in a voiceless close-up. And he continuously follows each timid step forward with a self-critical step backwards: "I cleaned the floor but did not do it well."

Of course, in the same years that Jaakko was posting his writings on DawsonsCreek.info, Sam Pulitzer and Mathieu Malouf were gaining currency for a related type of inconvenient commentary on their site jerrymagoo.blogspot.com. Authoring posts pseudonymously since 2009, they've been a more or less constant art world troll, singling out individuals, organizations, and trends with crude denunciations. Whereas Jaakko asks, "How to appear antagonistic enough to be credible while protecting fragile social relations?" Sam and Mathieu have confirmed that unbridled and seemingly indiscriminate antagonism is as good a way as any of gaining access to the discourse and historical lineage they were eager to be part of. The question remains, though, whether the hater culture that Sam and Mathieu nurtured and the paranoia and injury that comes along with it are actually reasonable replacements for the one of euphoric affirmation and convenient exclusion that both they and Jaakko seem to have taken issue with.

Jaakko's criticism is more elegant in its precision, if not in the desperation that it betrays—he'd call it his "thirstiness". After dropping out of art school in Helsinki, where he studied painting, and moving to Berlin, where he didn't continue to paint, Jaakko's tumblr became his focus. It was an archive for his work and a way of accessing something like a public. Nevertheless, post after post makes it clear that this fantasy participation online wasn't equivalent to the access that some of his peers were attaining through their inclusion in shows like 2011's Based in Berlin and the various forms of institutional and market validation that followed shortly thereafter. Jaakko responded with sincere doubt and dissatisfaction in the tenor of the 'New Sincerity'—the name for a strain of mid '80s–to–mid 2000s music and literature that opposed postmodern irony and cynicism—also the title of Jaakko's 2011 show at Future Gallery in Berlin. Think Conor Oberst lilting, "If I could act like this was my real life and not some cage where I've been placed, / well then, I could tell you the truth like I used to and not be afraid of sounding fake. / Now all that anyone is listening for are the mistakes."

Jaakko would rather point to Lindsay Zoladz's 2012 Pitchfork article "Mind is Your Might: Fiona Apple's Oversharing" about the '90s singer-songwriter's comeback tour:

I'm not saying that there is something universally 'feminine' about Fiona Apple's music, or that her songs inherently appeal to any one group of people more than another. But I do think the reason why some women and queer people feel an affinity with her music is that it displays the destabilizing power of 'oversharing', the strangely radical gesture of presenting your mind and your body and your life as it is—which is always going to provide more of a release to the people who've been cautioned against sharing those sorts of things in the past. "The thrill of [Apple's songs]," Nitsuh Abebe wrote after an Austin show, "is just a certain frankness about reality, and the sense of an artist who can cut casually to the core of what life is like." To me, the sudden triumph of her return exists in the same cultural moment as people sharing photos of gay couples who've just been married, or female protesters (hilariously) trolling Rick Perry's Facebook wall with questions about menstruation to protest his stance on reproductive health. It's the thrill of voices dismissed as silly or excessive in the past now deriving power from the ordinary details of their everyday lives.

In Jaakko's writing, the contemporary art world is a pretty shitty place handing out rejection, populated by sell-outs, and guilty of engendering feelings of inadequacy, doubt, embarrassment, and defeat. If this sounds like an exaggeration, that doesn't mean that it's not also sometimes true. Jaakko offers condemnations of the contemporary art world from the perspective of a well-informed outsider because, emotionally and psychologically, that's how it can sometimes feel. And he gives us a version of self-centrism and self-branding via the exposure of real thoughts, feelings, and experiences. That may not sound like much, but reading Scorched Earth shows that disclosing in this way is something different—and constructive—and in rare but fortunate cases also empowering.

I want to end with an email that I wrote to Jaakko. It sparked the conversation that led to me writing this afterword. It's about one of the more recent posts on Jaakko's tumblr. As someone who writes criticism myself, and someone inspired by what Jaakko does with his writing, I also thought it'd be a good excuse to open up a bit.

--

Jaako,

I started out wanting to write you an email, thinking that would loosen up my writing, since I can't write like you. But I ended up with this. If any of this is interesting to you, I'd be more than happy to make comments on your text given my perspective.

As I already mentioned, I was really moved by the post you wrote about being in London for Frieze, when you went with a group of friends to Wolfgang Tillmans's party and got turned away. I think this is a really valid place for criticism to come from, an 'outsider' perspective—in scare quotes because though in so many ways you're not an outsider, you felt like one, and feelings matter.

As I see it, Network Fatigue isn't forthcoming about the conditions of the network (both social and professional) that Pablo's addressing in it. For one thing, it's a network of people who have at times created power and cultural capital through exclusion, as happens in all networks. And it's frustrating to see someone within this network and with a certain type of power—to provide exposure through writing, to provide critical validation, and to inscribe into history—write about how tired they all are of networking, without acknowledging the privilege of power that they all enjoy.

These are people who are 'fatigued' by the networking that they've been hard at work at, and succeeding at, for some time. (The same goes for their relationship to a discourse about 'networks'.) In the case of some of these artists, it's a type of networking that's far and above—that's at times been closer to the exploitation of their peers, their audiences, and the cultural vernaculars that they have access to. That practice has become thoroughly accepted today, but this 'fatigue' is melodramatic, and doesn't serve their peers or their audiences or the vernacular cultures that they draw from. It just serves them. It isn't any more generous; it's just as exclusionary.

The irony is that this essay complaining about networking still serves the ends of networking: Writing about these artists at the exclusion of other artists is self-perpetuating and also provides them with exposure—as does all writing, of course, but the text doesn't own up to its own effects. Nor does it acknowledge what these artists are really reacting against: a status quo that they bought into, then remodeled for their immediate environment. Tobi was one of the earliest artists on Contemporary Art Daily insisting on the aesthetic of documentation that he's now subverting (and he's aware of that). Max and Calla drew in the crowd that their project needs in order to survive, and yet they retreat into spaces where the crowd isn't allowed to follow (though audiences are sometimes made aware of the spaces where they aren't invited and some of what goes on there).

If you ask me, the work needs to be seen through a lens of inclusion and exclusion, as well as the way that these artists have power and interact with power. For me, that's more to the point: These aesthetics and this rhetoric have an ideological function.

'Fatigue' is a natural foil for the affective labor of network capitalism, but here it just looks like another way of bolstering the

system in place and the present conditions. It's just dissatisfaction masking exclusion in a way that maintains power, rather than redistributing it.

Thanks for your text.

Hope to talk soon,
John